# PREPARING FOR PARTNERSHIP:

## STANDARD LOAN

UNLESS RECALLED BY ANOTHER READER
THIS ITEM MAY BE BORROWED FOR

### FOUR WEEKS

To renew, telephone:
01243 816089 (Bishop Otter)
01243 812099 (Bognor Regis)

Published in 1991
by the National Foundation for Educational Research,
The Mere, Upton Park, Slough, Berkshire SL1 2DQ

ISBN 0 7005 1300 0

# Contents

# The National Foundation for Educational Research

The National Foundation for Educational Research in England and Wales (NFER) was founded in 1946 and is Britain's leading educational research institution. NFER's main role is to carry out research and development projects in all sectors of the public educational system and in professional and vocational training.

NFER is an independent organisation. As such, its approach is scientific, apolitical and non-partisan. The expert and experienced staff of the Foundation make use of a wide range of modern research techniques in their work. By means of surveys, interviews and case studies, NFER has provided objective evidence for a variety of audiences such as teachers; education, health and social services workers; professional bodies; employers; and parents. In addition to projects determined by its members, it undertakes a large number of sponsored projects at the request of government departments, local authorities and individual professional organisations.

Examples of studies recently undertaken include: the organisation of LEA-based in-service training; the national evaluation of staff development and appraisal in further education; progression for students with special educational needs from school to further education; the education of children in care; training for work with the visually impaired; and an evaluation of new developments in nurse training.

# Acknowledgements

We would like to express our gratitude to everyone who has helped us with this research. In particular, we are indebted to the many individuals working in education, health, social services and the voluntary sector who were so generous in sharing their experiences with us, inviting us to attend meetings and allowing us to probe the setbacks and pitfalls of early attempts at inter-agency collaboration. Their commitment to their work, to their clients and to the principles of cooperation is encouraging and we wish them good luck in their future endeavours.

We would also like to thank members of the project's advisory group for their help in shaping the nature of the research and to extend special thanks to Jean McGinty for reading and commenting so constructively on the draft of this report.

Within the NFER we wish to thank Dr Seamus Hegarty for his encouragement and advice in shaping this report and his comments on the manuscript, the secretaries in the Professional Studies Department for their work on the draft version, Mary Hargreaves for her skillful work in preparing the report for publication and Tim Wright for the cover design.

## Note to the text

Finally, we recognise that we are probably as guilty as anyone when it comes to using terms and phrases favoured by our own profession. We apologise for the educational flavour the text inevitably bears. We have tried to keep this to a minimum and hope that despite this shortcoming, those from other backgrounds will find the report useful and relevant.

# I INTRODUCTION

## Background

It is thirteen years since the Warnock Committee recommended inter-agency collaboration as the most effective response in the long term to the wide range of individualised services required by people with special educational needs. The fundamental principle underpinning this recommendation was integration both in the educational system and in the wider community. It was recognised that the adoption of an integrationist policy would have important implications not only for the organisation and management of educational institutions, but also for the coordination of people's educational experiences with what was happening in other areas of their lives. In the intervening years it has become widely acknowledged that inter-agency support systems must be regarded as the essential infrastructure through which relevant education, training and employment plans are designed, implemented and monitored for those who have special needs.

Special needs can arise from physical disability, sensory impairment, learning difficulties, emotional or behavioural problems, or any combination of these. The kinds of support that individuals require to meet their special needs will clearly be correspondingly diverse. If for one reason or another this support is not available, they will be severely limited in their ability to benefit from the education and training opportunities that are on offer.

Research carried out during the 1980s suggested that the transition to adult life for young people with special needs was in fact characterised by reduced contact with the health and social services, lack of practical guidance and information, and widespread experience of gaps in or duplication of the necessary services (Castree and Walker, 1981; Hirst, 1983; Sills, 1987; Thomas and Bax, 1985). Individual needs were still being addressed by a series of fragmented responses that did not form part of an overall strategy. In recognition of this fact, the coordinated delivery of a wide range of services has been a major theme in recent national legislation. How far, then, has this legislation had an impact on professional practice, has it gone far enough, what factors tend to inhibit collaborative working, and to what extent are the various agencies beginning to espouse a new concept of partnership?

These are the central questions that were addressed in the research reported here. Its intention was to identify models of inter-agency working and examine them in practice; to ascertain how far they related to desired objectives in terms of supporting progression; and to draw from them lessons for developing good practice on a wider scale. As a starting point for the study, discussions were held with a range of professionals from education, health and the social services, who were asked to suggest local authority and college-based initiatives that might be regarded as exemplifying good practice. The first weeks of the research were then devoted to visiting the recommended locations to interview key personnel and to collect information on the origins and operation of each initiative.

As a result of these visits six locations were selected for case study investigation. They were chosen to represent differences in the scale and level of involvement of a range of services as well as management-led and grass roots-led origins. In each location interviews were held with individuals from the various agencies involved and, where possible, relevant meetings were attended. Documentation produced in connection with each initiative was also collected, including minutes of meetings and policy statements.

It soon became apparent that there were a number of common difficulties facing all those attempting to mount initiatives of this nature. There were significant elements of good practice associated with all of the initiatives, but none had succeeded in achieving its overall objective of embedding new working practices in the system as a whole. Despite all the rhetoric and exhortations to action made over the past thirteen years, despite the willingness and sheer hard work of individuals, inter-agency collaboration was obviously proving to be a hard nut to crack. The research therefore began to focus more directly on gaining a thorough understanding of the factors militating against progress in this area.

The report begins by setting out the state of play as it emerged from our research and from other recent investigations. It then goes on to describe the experiences of people in the case study locations and to suggest reasons why plans did or did not come to fruition. Finally it takes up a number of key topics emerging from the research and offers a series of questions which professionals may wish to address in seeking possible ways forward.

## The current context

The recent report from HMI (DES, 1991) on transition from school to further education (FE) for students with learning difficulties found that few local education authorities (LEAs) had set common objectives with other agencies and that small

3

localised initiatives were much more likely to exist than strategic inter-agency planning at senior management level. Inter-agency work was described as fragmented and limited to the legislative requirements associated with the Disabled Persons Act 1986 and the Annual Review procedures of the Education Act 1981.

Even at this level, evidence from other studies would suggest that progress in implementing legislative requirements has been slow. For example, the improvement of coordination between social services departments (SSDs) and LEAs was an important intention of the Disabled Persons Act 1986. A number of the Sections of the Act have still to become operational - notably those relating to advocacy, consultation and collaboration - but Sections 5 and 6 concerned with school leavers were implemented in 1988. A report from the Social Services Inspectorate (1990a) noted: 'The Act served the invaluable functions - some 17 years after the Chronically Sick and Disabled Persons Act - of raising the profile of disabled people, of legislating afresh for their needs and those of their carers, and of providing a legislative framework for good practice.' However, the intention of the Act does not yet appear to have had an impact on any significant scale. For instance, under the Act the SSD must appoint an 'appropriate officer' who is required to give an opinion as to whether a young person referred to them by the LEA is a 'disabled person'. The SSI report found that in half of their sample of SSDs the people appointed to carry out these assessments were occupational therapy staff. The report notes that this could 'militate against a comprehensive assessment that takes a range of physical, medical, emotional and social factors into account' and goes on to suggest a broader assessment drawing in social workers, other SSD personnel, and staff from the health and education services. A second report from the SSI (1990b) focused on inspections carried out in six local authorities. Effective links between SSDs and LEAs were found to be extremely variable and only one had in place a notification procedure that met the requirements of the Act.

The Care in the Community initiative has the potential to offer appropriate packages to young people but is at present focusing on the immediate problem of supporting adults moving from long-stay hospitals.

The Education Act 1981 does not require LEAs to provide support for students attending FE colleges and even where LEAs decided to offer advisory and inspectorial services to FE, the demands made upon these services by the schools are in practice given priority. Moreover, the HMI report (op.cit.) suggested that such demands were placing increasing pressure on services attempting to fulfil their legislative duty under the statements procedures of the Act. Even within the same local authority, individual students making the transition to FE could not be guaranteed equal opportunity. Whether or not they received appropriate support seemed to depend on the luck of the draw rather than on an overall policy for special needs. A similar situation obtains in relation to social workers and specialist careers officers, the number of whose clients can vary enormously even in authorities of the same size.

Part of the problem in providing a comprehensive service lies in the fact that the legislation itself is originating in different Government departments. What has emerged to date is, then, a piecemeal solution that offers neither a coherent policy framework nor centralised guidance on how collaborative action is to be achieved. Added to this is the fact that the education, health and social services are at present all facing fundamental changes in their own internal structures and working practices. If inter-agency work is not central to anyone's job, it is difficult to see how practitioners can give it the priority it deserves.

At the level of individual colleges and schools, HMI (op.cit.) noted the dependence of inter-agency links on individual efforts and goodwill rather than on a coordinated approach. Several schools were reported to be acting independently in making links with other agencies in the absence of guidance on this matter from their LEA, while college tutors were using personal contacts to access services for their students. While such a strategy may work as a short-term measure, it has a number of intrinsic shortcomings. Consulting other agencies on an individual basis is time-consuming and takes teachers away from their other activities; a change of personnel can mean the collapse of existing channels of communication; and the lack of formal structures for arranging appropriate support imposes serious limitations on the range of students who can achieve access to FE.

The fact that this is often the only strategy used by colleges fits squarely with the development of special needs work in FE. In general, the impetus for establishing provision came from individuals and a coordinated whole college approach has been difficult to achieve. The formulation of detailed policy statements and the appointment of named persons to secure their implementation represent important steps towards this. Nevertheless, a study undertaken for the FEU (Bradley and Pocklington, 1990) found that many senior college managers were seen by their staff as lacking sufficient understanding of what was entailed in providing for students with special needs. With a few notable exceptions, they failed to appreciate that curriculum delivery involved a substantial level of liaison with a wide range of professionals and that this took time. While liaison work is usually written into the job description of the special needs coordinator, the variety of other tasks that he or she is required to perform makes effective inter-agency working an unrealistic expectation. Hutchinson (1985) noted that the responsibilities of the coordinator typically embraced:

## Teaching

* *Small groups* - possibly teaching students in the areas of literacy, numeracy and language development to support the development of other aspects of the course programme.

* *Individuals* - offering individualised support to students perhaps on a remedial basis.

## Support

* *Students* - establishing regular communication with college staff in academic, vocational and other areas on the progress and problems of individual students and dealing with these on an individual or group basis.

* *Staff* - assisting college staff to recognise the special needs of students and to manage these effectively in the teaching situation.

## Assessment and evaluation

* *Students* - monitoring the progress of students, developing diagnostic-prescriptive assessment, identifying learning styles, current performance levels,

specific strengths and difficulties and assuming the main responsibility for the modification of existing plans whenever necessary.

* *Staff* - assisting college staff in developing appropriate evaluation procedures both in initial and on-going assessment and in coordinating with staff over the written reporting and recording of student progress.

## Curriculum development

* Being involved in the development of individualised educational programmes, seeing this process through its design, implementation, evaluation and revision stages. In particular to advise on teaching strategies, materials and equipment, having regard for the expected general principles and behavioural outcomes of the educational programmes.

## Guidance/liaison

* *Students* - conferring regularly with students regarding their educational programmes and their personal problems and difficulties; being on hand to help in situations where students create difficulties in the college or other environments, particularly with regard to behaviour and related problems.

* *Staff* - acting as student advocate and mediator with other college staff in their management of students. This may involve direct negotiation with departmental and senior college management as well as dealing with non-teaching staff.

* *Schools* - obtaining and supplying information on curricula and assessment; attending school leavers'

case conferences and social functions; possibly participating in joint in-service training.

* *Parents* - providing regular communication, both written and verbal, to parents on the progress of students and acting as student advocate in the interface between college and home.

* *Support agencies* - identifying and securing the services of support agencies relevant to each students' needs; monitoring and maintaining the progress of this intervention.

* *Post-college placements* - establishing links with adult education, voluntary and YTS schemes, adult training centres, employers and so on.

Thus, for most colleges, liaison with other professionals tends to take place in a relatively *ad hoc* way and, apart from the formal setting of the case conference, continues to rely on informal personal contacts made by individual course tutors attempting to meet the immediate needs of a particular student or group of students. They, too, have little time to undertake this work. Their task would be made much easier if they were to have recourse to an existing liaison network, already established between the college and support agencies in the local community. As it stands, recent government initiatives designed to remove FE colleges from the control of the local authorities are likely to make contacting services even more problematic.

Failure to achieve a coordinated service results in waste of resources, duplication of effort and a hit or miss situation where some some get a fair deal while others do not. At the heart of all this effort is the individual who can be faced at one extreme with a plethora of conflicting advice and at the other with the realisation that the necessary support is simply not available.

Our investigation encountered numerous examples of coordinators and course tutors making intermittent contact with colleagues in the support agencies. They did not amount to coherent inter-agency working. It is, however, important to put these initiatives in their historical context. At the time of the publication of the Warnock report there were very few students with special needs actually in the colleges. The FE sector has come a very long way since then in terms both of student numbers and of the range of provision that is on offer. The calls now being made for greater inter-agency collaboration represent one more stage in a developmental process that is aiming to provide equal opportunities for all to fulfil their potential in education, employment and society.

Multi-agency working is not, then, an end in itself. Rather it is a means to a much wider objective. The findings from our research draw upon the experiences of professionals who are attempting to work in partnership with colleagues in other services. We offer them as a basis for discussion.

# II PROBLEMS WITH INTER-AGENCY COOPERATION

As we have indicated, relatively few examples of wholly successful inter-agency collaboration were found. However, this is not particularly surprising since comprehensive multi-agency working is by no means easy to achieve. The reasons for this are numerous and often interrelated. The main ones are explored below, using examples encountered in the course of our research to illustrate common problems which arose.

## Slow progress towards joint policy development

Probably the most serious hindrance to inter-agency working at the present time is the almost total lack of joint policy development across agencies. Without the support of a joint policy which bridges the boundaries between the various statutory and voluntary bodies individuals' attempts to establish links across agencies are inevitably limited. Joint policy-making is the essential ingredient needed to provide coherence and support to these individual efforts. Since special needs provision is not necessarily age-related, the key words in policy formulation must be continuity and progression. For some people a lifetime of provision will be needed involving different agencies at different transitional points.

The development of a joint policy would help to clarify common aims between agencies and resolve differences at senior level so that those working within each agency would have a clear understanding of what they are working towards.

It would facilitate a more client-centred approach, enabling the rationalisation of provision to provide coordinated services. Moreover, with a joint policy in place, workers who might otherwise not consider working in partnership with other agencies would find it harder to ignore the fact that this is an important aspect of their job. It is widely acknowledged that when the commitment of senior management is seen to be present, other agencies are more likely to take liaison seriously on the understanding that the necessary decision-making structures to back their actions will be in place.

However, no examples of authority-wide, inter-agency policy documents were found. While the existence of joint policy statements cannot, in themselves, ensure that cooperation takes place, they can provide an important framework in which developments are encouraged and supported through early difficulties and maintained once they become established.

## EXAMPLE

In one area, individual practitioners from health, social services and education had formed a special needs liaison group. However, they felt their efforts were undermined because senior managers were not getting together to make policy decisions. They felt that the lack of discussion between policy makers meant that the current ad hoc provision for people with special needs would continue, and despite their own efforts at coordination, rationalisation of services would not happen. Transport problems, for example, were felt to be something which regularly caused problems for clients which workers could do very little about.

The community care manager described a recent example where the absence of authority-wide agreed policy had meant that opportunities for smoothing the transition of two eighteen-year-olds from school to a day centre had been lost. The two students were about to leave a local special school. However, it was not until June, as term was about to end, that the school contacted social services to say that the two young men would be moving on to the local day centre. The community care manager was very concerned: first, that there had been no real planning for the two; and secondly, that insufficient time was available for useful transition arrangements to be made. Instead, a meeting was hastily set up between himself, a social worker who was new to the cases, a teacher from the special school, the young men and their parents. There was only time for one visit to the day centre and a worker from the day centre visited the school on the last day of term. The move to the day centre proved to be a traumatic one for the young men and their families, particularly as transport arrangements had also been muddled.

The community care manager said that a much smoother transition could have been achieved with proper coordination. He believed that what was needed was a policy agreement between education and social services stating that a social worker must be involved in all 14-plus reviews so that planning for the future could start early. This would have allowed plenty of time to consider various options and, if the day centre was felt to be the most appropriate, the young men could have made several visits there before starting full time. Also, the key worker from the day centre would have had the opportunity of spending time with the young men in their special school to become familiar with their abilities, performance, curriculum and so on and to discuss the transition with their teachers.

## EXAMPLE

In another location, although senior managers in health, education and social services had begun to acknowledge the need for them to liaise over policy, the importance of involving all relevant agencies did not seem to have been recognised. The outcome, therefore, was still a fragmented approach to policy development. For example, the new director of social services was reported to have identified a need for a 'corporate policy' which had led to social services and health services inviting one another's representatives to high level meetings. The education department, for its part, had set up the *Post-16 Special Needs Advisory Group* which was looking at ways of rationalising previously ad hoc provision. The outcome of the group's early work was a draft report *Special Needs Post-16*. This report described how it had attempted to deal with the need to collaborate with other agencies:

> *In approaching its task the group was aware of the limitations of its own knowledge and expertise, the scale of the review it was asked to undertake and the responsibilities of other organisations and agencies in the web of provision for special educational needs, e.g. the health authority and social services department. It therefore requested written (our emphasis) submissions from providing establishments, service and statutory authorities with responsibilities for children, young people and adults with special educational needs.*

However, among the report's recommendations was the proposal to set up a support team which could provide access to the range of professionals working in the field of post-16 provision:

> *A comprehensive post-16 support team organised on a federal basis across the city's colleges should be developed to offer support to students with special needs. The support team should offer skilled counselling and access to specialist services such as those provided by educational psychologists, careers service, social services department and district health authority. This team should work collaboratively with other relevant support mechanisms.*

It also identified a job in coordinating the range of service provision across the authority:

> *It is necessary for the authority to recognise the magnitude of the task in developing and coordinating*

*a comprehensive network of provision for post-16 special needs, particularly in view of the variety of agencies involved as service-providers. Consideration should be given to the creation of a senior post within the authority with the post-holder assuming responsibility for developing school-college links, individual college provision, interdepartmental coordination, federal initiatives and provision of staff development.*

But this was as far as the report went in urging inter-agency connections. Above all, the opportunity to work with other agencies to produce a **joint** report was lost.

Another example of the failure to involve all agencies in joint policy-making arose when the education and social services departments started meetings to prepare a joint statement on their goals for services for people with special needs. It was intended to be for clients and client pressure groups, to provide improved information about the range of provision and what the objectives of the two agencies were. Senior level people, including the deputy director of social services and the senior assistant director (further and higher education), were involved in drafting the statement but, although the statement covered health service provision, the health authority had not been consulted. There was some suggestion that a subgroup might be formed later to consider the statement and it was felt that this might be an appropriate time to involve the health authority. The rationale for this was that they were not seeking a joint venture with the health authority, only their support for the statement. This was because education and social services were departments of the city council, unlike health.

## Structures at local authority level

The logical progression from joint policy development involves taking steps to ensure that structures at local authority level facilitate, rather than obstruct, such a policy. The way in which individual jobs or whole services are organised can obviously affect the way in which people work and the opportunities created for inter-agency cooperation. Therefore, unless there is a commitment to address the differences between agencies and the problems that may stem from them, a joint policy will not, of course, bring about change. Moreover, individuals who work within each of the agencies will need to support the changes which are being proposed. They need to be able to see the benefits which can be derived and to understand how their job fits into the overall pattern of service provision. Other professional differences are covered in later sections, but the following examples indicate the types of structure at local authority level in which inter-agency collaboration is effectively discouraged and where institutionalised competition and mistrust between agencies can operate.

## EXAMPLE

Stephen was the health service coordinator when the Care in the Community initiative was just getting under way. In attempting to work with social services over this, he experienced difficulties in marrying the approach of the two agencies. His main criticism was that the social services department was too bureaucratic and had been slow to respond to new proposals. As a consequence, the health authority had looked to the education department and the voluntary sector when setting up the new arrangements. This had upset social services who saw such moves as impinging on their territory.

Part of the problem was the difference in the structure of the health and social services. The Care in the Community coordinator felt the former was governed by principles of general management, with few committees, while the social services spent months discussing the sort of proposal and scheme they wanted, only to find that at the committee stage it might not be supported financially. Also, there were now three-year contracts for general managers in the health service. This lent itself to a different attitude to tackling the issues within the health authority and contrasted with what the coordinator described as the 'municipal way of working'. Another element was the ten-year strategy which the health authority had, which was subject to annual review. Finally, there were differences between the social and health services in terms of their role as providers. The health service saw its role as buying in expertise, operating as agent purchasing services for its clients, whereas social services had traditionally run its own services and been direct service providers.

The social services manager responsible for liaising with the health service took much the same view. He felt that social services reorganisation and reform was needed, in particular, the decentralisation of decision-making in order to get things done more quickly. He described the minefield he had to tread in achieving decisions and the many subcommittees which had to be consulted before action could be taken. Explaining why the social services department had been so slow to respond to joint initiatives with the health authority over Care in the Community, he said that the council saw it as the health authority embarking on a cost-cutting exercise, dashing into new initiatives without the necessary infrastructure being set up first. However, he was hopeful that changes in personnel at the top would start to make relations easier.

He, too, felt the differences in the structures themselves were having an adverse affect and contrasted the health authority's ten-year plan with the social services' urban programme; the two did not link up. Scope for joint working at senior management level was therefore lost because the two hierarchies were running parallel, but separately. Yet health and social services each saw themselves as having the principal role in coordinating service provision.

A further problem was that health authority and local authority boundaries were not the same; thus the social services department was only in communication with one of the three health authorities which dealt with its clients.

These differences in structures appeared to work against a unified form of approach between the agencies. Historical differences were making the process of bridge-building difficult, even where the will now seemed to exist to develop new ways of working together.

Moreover, the motivation for joint working seemed at times to stem from a desire to secure funding, rather than from a commitment to a new partnership in providing services for people with special needs.

## EXAMPLE

Arising from the Care in the Community initiative was a three-year pilot scheme proposal in which 24 clients from a psychiatric hospital would attend a local FE college daily. Initially, two college lecturers were to attend the hospital two days per week to prepare the clients for the transition to college. When these people transferred to college, they were to be supported by a team comprising the two college lecturers and five care assistants. Supplementary help was to be provided by physiotherapists and occupational therapists who would visit the college when needed. It was envisaged that access to college would be supported by community nursing trainees and the setting up of a student befriending scheme in the college. An implementation group had been established to oversee the introduction of the pilot scheme. It involved college staff, hospital staff (senior level and practitioners) and a health authority manager.

However, the social services department was very much against this proposal. Its representatives expressed concerns that the scheme would merely involve the setting up of a social education centre (SEC) equivalent in the college and that the college was using the initiative as a means of solving its falling roll problem. The college believed the real reason for social services' objections stemmed from a concern that money from Care in the Community was going to the college and not to social services. However, despite these differences, social services was prepared to support the proposal at the Joint Consultative Committee meeting because it was about to seek the health authority's support for a similar proposal to close one of its SECs.

The voluntary sector, too, came up against these inter-agency rivalries. The following example illustrates how once again the competition for the same client group was at the heart of the problem.

## EXAMPLE

In this town there was a charity-run day centre which organised activities for people in the community, some of which were specifically designed for those deemed to have special needs. The activities organiser felt that the centre's links with the social services department had always been poor. In her view the difficulties had arisen due to power struggles and personalities. The social services department made a contribution to the running of the centre in the form of an annual grant. Apart from knowing how the money was spent there was little contact. However, social services workers had recently started to take more of an interest and relations had gradually started to thaw. Social services and the voluntary centre were beginning to recognise each other's contribution and links were being made which benefited individual clients.

The Mencap officer in the same town reported a similarly uneasy relationship with social services while the former director was in post. She felt that he had discouraged liaison, while paying lip-service to it, and that this had had repercussions down the line. Now, under a new director, relations were improving steadily and regular liaison had been set up.

These earlier difficulties were confirmed by social services workers. Their former director had seen a role for social services as the main provider of services which the voluntary sector was encroaching upon. However, they thought the shift in policy was only partly to do with their new director, believing the Griffiths report to have had some influence also. Voluntary agencies were being encouraged to develop their services and together with health were being seen as providers of services while the social services department was seeking more of a coordinating role.

Another factor which can affect collaborative efforts is the way in which services are organised. Sometimes problems arise because too many people have responsibility for liaison, leading to confusion and lack of coordination. It seems that within a unit or team it is important for one person to have overall responsibility for liaision, or at least for one person to have an overview. Where this is lacking, problems and misunderstandings appear to arise more easily, as the following example shows.

## EXAMPLE

In this location, the careers service comprised four careers officers; three general workers and one with sole responsibility for students with special educational needs. It was found that this system worked well until the person was on leave or ill at which time there was no-one to contact about careers advice for those with special educational needs. Consequently, the service was reorganised and all the work, including the responsibility for special schools, was divided equally between each of the four careers officers. However, the change was found to have backfired, since there were too many people to liaise with now and no one person who had an overview. Thus they had exchanged one set of problems for another.

A further aspect of local authority structures which can inhibit liaison is the limitation placed on workers by their age-related job remits or the constraining nature of a client-group label, such as MLD or SLD. For most, these difficulties are recognised and efforts are made to overcome them; indeed a blurring of the edges, strictly speaking breaking the rules, can often be the outcome. This is a problem nevertheless, because while some workers will be prepared to do this, others are less willing on the grounds that the scope of their involvement could become infinitely more complex, and their workload therefore greater.

## Initiating links

Initiating links between agencies can happen at any level and at any time. The main motivation appears to stem from a recognition that inter-agency liaison is an important factor in achieving the best services for people with special needs. However, the spur to seeking links often seems to be the requirement to respond to a new set of circumstances. At senior management level this might be new legislation, a change in agency policy or a new appointment. More commonly, at practitioner level, initiatives usually occur in response to such things as being in a new job and feeling in need of information or support, the introduction of a new college course or an immediate problem with a particular student or group of students. The following example is typical of the type of grass roots initiative which commonly occurs.

### EXAMPLE

Jane was recently appointed, from outside the borough, to a newly created post as special needs coordinator at the FE college. In the absence of any obvious network, either within or outside the college, she made contact initially with her counterpart in a neighbouring college who was also new to the borough. A year later these two college coordinators described their connections with other professionals as still very patchy. Part of the problem, they felt, was that the authority did not have a policy regarding inter-agency collaboration and therefore when they took up their posts no formal contacts existed with other professional groups working in the same field, often with the same clients. Jane spoke to her college principal about this, explaining that it would be necessary to build up links with other professional groups to support the work done in the college. As a direct consequence, the principal got together with the principal in the neighbouring college and together they approached health and social services.

This led to the decision to form what became known as the *Special Needs Liaison Group* which involved just four key people: the two colleges' special needs coordinators, the district planning officer from the health authority and the social services management officer (mental handicap service development). The rationale for such a small group was that there was a need for a close-knit team which would be able to make decisions. The feeling was that a larger group might not achieve very much. It was intended that the group would expand as the need arose. Members worked well together and were committed to putting in the extra work needed.

The group set out to identify what was currently available in the borough for people with special needs over the age of 16 years. Their aims were to avoid duplication of provision, rationalise services and, above all, ensure that nobody was falling through the gaps between services. An early problem was identified as being poor liaison with the SECs and voluntary agencies. The social services representative therefore invited the managers of some SECs and voluntary agencies to attend the meetings on a regular basis. However, the attendance of these new people did not immediately resolve the problem of poor communications with the SECs; differences in expectations and interpretations of concepts such as 'progression' were seen to create rifts between the different groups represented.

Nevertheless, some of the positive outcomes of this initial liaison period were identified as:

- The profile of FE special needs provision was raised. Though there was no borough-wide post-16 special needs policy, the colleges' role in provision for special educational needs was acknowledged and the two college coordinators were consulted more by the education authority.

- Communication with the voluntary agencies and SECs improved.

- Ideas were formulated for planning staff development sessions involving a range of professional groups, although finding the time to organise such activities was a problem with only one full time member of staff involved in special needs at each college.

- A place for each of the colleges' special needs coordinators on two of the Care in the Community joint planning teams was negotiated by the health authority representative.

## Identifying the right people

Links are often sought by workers who are new to a job, sometimes even a locality, and therefore may not know whether a network already exists, or who would be the most useful people to contact. Lists of names and addresses of contact people, should they exist, are often out of date and the worker has to start afresh. Even where the worker has been in post for some time, however, the isolation between agencies can be such that identifying useful link people in other agencies is still a problem. Partly this is because knowing the 'right' person relies to a great extent on understanding what the work of other agencies and individuals involves. If such knowledge is lacking, a kind of Catch 22 scenario may exist: people are not contacted because not enough is known about what they do, yet this is because they are not in contact! Furthermore, if a liaison meeting is being planned it is important to invite all relevant parties. Overlooking someone in the first round of meetings can be interpreted as a snub and may cause difficulties in developing new relationships between agencies.

Devising a plan of a local network is often seen as an initial target of liaison groups, helping them to identify what provision is available, being duplicated, or non-existent. The liaison group described in the following example had set out to do this, but experienced difficulties because they did not have all the necessary people in the group to provide the information they needed.

## EXAMPLE

The liaison group had spent several meetings drawing up a flowchart showing the range of provision in the borough for adults with special needs. They aimed to include details of type of provision (e.g. day centre, specialist advice), numbers of places, opportunities for progression, location, contact name and telephone number. It was envisaged that this would:

- serve as a useful way for the liaison group to combine their shared local knowledge and identify gaps in provision;

- provide useful information to everyone working with adults with special needs in the borough; and

- be used by clients and parents as a useful reference point when exploring the opportunities available to them within the locality.

However, throughout the exercise of producing a flowchart, it was recognised that not all the people were present who were needed to provide the details required. They decided to fill in what they could for the time being and follow this up with a questionnaire to each provider of day services asking for details such as number of places, funding source, whether residential or not, criteria for accepting clients, age range, ability and type of clients catered for.

At a subsequent meeting, the group reviewed the people who were felt to be missing, beyond those needed for the task of completing the flowchart. It was hoped that the new adviser for special educational needs would be prepared to attend the meetings. The current one, who was about to retire, had chosen not to become involved, even though FE was part of his remit. The group felt this was because he was only interested in schools.

They also planned to invite a representative from the community mental health team. Another concern was to have representation from the residential homes, but they did not want someone from every home in case the group became too big. They decided the Mencap representative would be sufficient to provide an overview of this side of things.

Identifying people in this way the group was hoping to develop a sense of identity. It made a conscious decision not to invite representatives from special schools, even though they were recognised as important, because they wanted to keep the group very much as an FE/SEC link group.

## Persuading others of the need for inter-agency collaboration

Where people indicate a reluctance to become involved in collaboration it is usually blamed on workload and lack of time. Certainly these are real problems which need to be considered by service managers. However, there can be more to it than this. Do the workers in other agencies see any benefit from establishing or maintaining links? Have they been involved in links before which have foundered? Are there historical differences between the agencies which make the person wary of becoming involved? Does the person share common goals with the workers in other agencies? Does the person put collaboration high enough on their list of priorities to make time for meetings? Do they feel threatened by the prospect of talking about their job and sharing information - is there a fear of being judged? Where a reluctance to forge links is encountered, for whatever reason, the chances are that the person trying to initiate (or maintain) links does not have the authority to insist on participation. This is where a formal policy might help the individuals to recognise inter-agency cooperation as part of their job.

## EXAMPLE

In one area, a special needs group had been set up which involved college tutors, representatives from the voluntary sector and SEC staff. However, after a relatively short period of time the attendance of some of the SEC representatives started to decline. The group were concerned at this apparent lack of interest. Although the departure of the social services day care manager was felt to be partly to blame, there was also felt to be a problem in not having a named person in each SEC who was the link person with the group. They decided to ask each SEC to nominate someone rather than have different people attending each time. It was recognised that this might seem an excessive burden on one worker in each SEC but the lack of continuity caused by having different representatives was felt to exacerbate the problem of poor attendance. Also, the group had reason to believe that in some centres minutes of their meetings were getting lost or left on SEC managers' desks and not passed on for all staff to read. It was also decided that 'regular' members of the group would each take a few of the SECs whose attendance had declined and phone them to try to encourage their renewed attendance.

## Maintaining links when people move on

Inevitably, people move jobs and links are perhaps more likely to break down at this stage than at any other. This is what happened in two of the locations visited in our research.

### EXAMPLE

The liaison group met with early setbacks: after six months two of the key people - the social services link person and the health services link person - moved on to new jobs. Losing these members of the core group was exacerbated by difficulties in finding replacements from the health and social services. Regarding the latter, the new postholder would have been willing to become involved, but was not permitted to do so because the remit of the job had narrowed which, together with the imminent reorganisation of the social services department, left FE low on the list of priorities. With the core group thus severely diminished, the liaison group suffered a loss of impetus. Meetings became less frequent and were poorly attended, in particular, by some of the SEC leaders. Despite all attempts to encourage these people to continue attending, including phone calls being made before meetings and minutes sent afterwards, only one or two remained at the end of the first year. It seems that the absence of the social services representative was directly linked to the SEC leaders finding the group less relevant.

### EXAMPLE

Carol was in charge of a special educational needs 16+ unit at the FE college. She had taken over this job 18 months earlier and, being new and feeling the need to know more about what was going on, set about contacting colleagues in other agencies in the locality. As it happened, there were several new people in the area who were equally keen to take the opportunity to meet regularly. The multi-professional link group which stemmed from this initiative met termly to discuss matters arising, including updating of personnel. It also usually identified a topic for discussion at each meeting, sometimes inviting guest speakers. The meetings lasted for about an hour in the early evening and locations were rotated between participants. Carol took notes of the meetings and circulated these to all members of the group which included: the community education officer, a representative from the adult training centre, a teacher from a local special school, a specialist careers officer, two community placement officers, three representatives from the YTS, and the county special needs coordinator. Once the group was established it set about drawing up a flowchart of the range of provision, contact names and telephone numbers. However, it emerged subsequently that Carol's predecessor had already set up a similar group which seemed to have lapsed with her departure. Thus the new postholder started the process over again.

Clearly if links are not formalised in some way it is difficult for new people to tap into an existing network. Moreover, the group may be relatively new or encountering difficulties and find it all too easy to disband. Therefore, leaving responsibility for liaison entirely up to individuals is leaving too much to chance.

What can be done about this? First, the network needs to be formally recognised by the local authority. This points again to the need for a multi-agency policy which makes collaboration a prerequisite of good practice. Secondly, there needs to be an up-to-date system of record keeping, with current names, addresses, phone numbers and details of the work and roles of the various members of the network. Reinventing the wheel every so many years is not a rational use of individual workers' time or resources and is among the many frustrations of inter-agency work. Thirdly, operating as part of an area-wide multi-professional team needs to be recognised as part of the job and built in to individual workers' job descriptions.

Another problem which is harder to plan for is the loss of impetus some groups suffer when a person who has had a pivotal role in bringing people together leaves. Again, if responsibility for liaison is written into the job description this can help, though it will not go all the way to solving the problem. A review of responsibilities would help individuals to recognise that roles within the group are going to have to be shifted. It will be particularly important for those who arrange meetings and/or provide written notes of meetings to pass on this information to the new person in post or to another member of the group. If the person who has departed was the one holding it all together on a motivational level too, perhaps it is a time for the group to have a thorough evaluation of its goals. Is everyone getting something out of the link? What have been the positive outcomes so far? Do any steps need to be taken to put the group on course again? Is a different type of liaison needed? Are there other people who need to be invited?

## Identifying common goals

An important aspect of collaboration between professional groups is agreement over aims and objectives. Very often it seems that people working with the same client group but in different agencies do not share the same goals. Sometimes this is an initial problem which means people see no point in getting together in the first place, but for others this realisation can come late in the day, often after several months of meetings. Such differences are not easily overcome and there is often a tendency at this stage for entrenched views and professional differences to emerge. Commonly the disagreements arise over differing beliefs about what would be best for the client. The following two examples are typical.

## EXAMPLE

An early development arising from one liaison group was the setting up of various SEC/college link courses. However, one of the main concerns the college coordinators had about this initiative was the issue of keeping SEC places open for students - something which the SECs were reluctant to do. While college tutors hoped that most students would have had opportunities for progression while on the link courses and would go on to further courses, or possibly employment, they wanted to ensure that places at the SECs would be kept open for students should these be needed. Although they believed that to return to the SEC after finishing a college course would be likely to result in much of the progress which had been made being lost, they thought this option was preferable to not having anything to do at all but stay home all day becoming depressed. Therefore, they were at pains to point out that they would not recommend that students return to their SEC unless there had been no progression while at college.

They felt, however, that it was unreasonable for SECs to fill the vacant place before the outcome of the college experience became known. They saw this as losing a facility for the student; one of their possible options gone, since clearly not all students make it into further training or employment. Moreover, college staff were aware of the concern of parents over this issue. While most parents were happy for their son or daughter to attend college, and even those not initially keen were won over by the positive effect such attendance was usually seen to have, they were nevertheless concerned that some form of permanent day provision be guaranteed, no matter what the outcome of the college experience. If by attending a short course at the college their son or daughter lost the permanent place at an SEC, the parent was likely to refuse a college placement.

The SEC leaders felt differently about this. In most circumstances they did not feel that returning to an SEC was appropriate for people who had been on one of the college courses. One of the SEC leaders indicated three reasons for this. First, the general ability level of people in the SECs was lower than it used to be because the more able were being 'creamed off' to participate in other forms of provision such as vocational training, college courses, Pathway initiatives and so on. This meant that those returning from college courses no longer had an appropriate peer group among SEC clients. Secondly, he felt that if people had been identified as being able to benefit from educational opportunities such as college courses, then the college should not be looking to send the student back to an SEC, but rather on to some other form of provision which would provide opportunities for progression. Thirdly, he felt that finding people work, and thus giving them the opportunity during the day for increased independence, responsibility for money and so on, only to return to a residential institution where they had no autonomy and could not spend the money they had earned was the wrong way to approach individual needs. In their view, the living arrangements should be tackled first, i.e. considering whether some form of independent living was feasible/appropriate before going on to look at training and work opportunities. Added to these concerns was the pressure the SECs were having to face from clients coming out of long-stay hospitals through Care in the Community. Therefore they needed all the spare places they had.

It was recognised by both the college and the SECs that this whole debate was related to the wider issue of opportunities for progression, or lack of them. The problem of finding such opportunities for the majority of students finishing college courses was identified by the liaison group as a key issue. It was agreed that there was a need for an assessment after a two-year college course between college staff and social services workers to look at further educational opportunities and leisure as well as employment. In the current situation, social activities were often the only link with the network of services after a college course had ended. Moreover, the group was aware of how crucial good liaison between the different professional groups was at stages of transition. It was felt that the DRO was sometimes instrumental in forging links at such times, but that this was a hit or miss situation very often.

31

The group reached a short-term compromise over these differences. It was agreed that some students would be able to go back to their SEC after a college course, or even at the same time as attending college, e.g. spending 21 hours per week at college, thereby not losing out on state benefits, and spending one day per week at the SEC. However, the college coordinator saw this as 'testing the water' to see how the arrangement would work out - generally there was still a lot of unhappiness among SEC leaders about this.

## EXAMPLE

The social services had become concerned that what had originally been a welcome initiative on the part of a local college to take some individuals from one of the SECs and offer them college courses was being undermined because students were getting stuck on a merry-go-round of college courses which offered them no progression. Furthermore, the fact that college places were being blocked by the first cohort of students meant that others could not have access to this opportunity. One of the social services managers associated with the link felt that this was negating all it had been set up to do. Although he felt that returning to the SEC would be boring for the students after the college, he also believed that education in perpetuity was a bad thing: 'there is no reason why people need education all their lives.' He took the view that other people in society do not use the college sector in this way and it was unreasonable of the college to assume that these students would have to because there seemed to be no alternative for them. What was needed was a way of making opportunities available after college.

He went on to suggest that the community services team should produce an annual report on the college initiative. This, he felt, would provide an overview which individual workers in different agencies could not attain alone. This in turn made strategic planning difficult: 'If we could all have a day out of our normal working lives occasionally to join forces for planning purposes, this would help everyone in their planning within agencies.' He gave as an example transport;

this often caused rows between the education department and social services over who should provide it. The education department would not provide transport once students were no longer in educational provision.

## Finding a common language

Another important professional difference emerges in the language used by different agencies. Terms such as 'normalisation' and 'assessment' can mean quite different things depending on who is using them. Even at the level of national legislation, differences in terminology are apparent which have important implications for the availability and delivery of coordinated services. The Education Act 1981 defines people with 'special educational needs' as those who have a difficulty in learning which calls for educational provision that is additional to, or otherwise different from, the provision made generally in schools. By contrast, the National Assistance Act 1948 offers a narrower definition of 'disability' which is related neither to learning difficulties nor to educational provision. This has resulted in a position whereby the number of young people who are the subject of a statement of special educational need and the number of those considered by the social services to be disabled can be radically different. Those with moderate learning difficulties or emotional and behavioural problems seem especially likely to fall through the net when appropriate service provision is being allocated. There is currently no systematic evidence on how the concepts of 'special educational need' and 'disability' correspond or on the consequences of their lack of fit for the young people concerned.

On the question of what is meant by 'assessment', college staff participating in this research pointed to two main differences between their own approach and that of the health and social services. First, they felt that colleagues in both health and social services carried out assessments as a matter of course, even if nothing specific was expected to follow from them, whereas the crucial question for FE staff was: assessment for what purpose? Secondly, they believed that social services and health workers made assessments at every stage of dealing with their clients, including initial assessments prior to any action being taken. College staff, on the other hand, might well prefer to work with a student for some time and, in the process of doing this, the assessment would evolve.

## Conditions of employment

Differences in conditions of employment between professional groups is another area which can cause problems. Considerable variations in hours, salaries and holiday entitlements exist, as do differences in working practices, such as the extent of personal autonomy in organising what is done and when. These factors can lead to aggrieved feelings on the part of those who think that their conditions and work situations compare unfavourably. Such dissatisfactions are not conducive to good inter-agency relations. Similar difficulties emerge in relation to training. This is often perceived as being high status or low status, judged on such elements as the length of the training, whether it is on-the-job training or college/university based, how empirical or factual the professional 'knowledge base' is, whether or not a formal qualification is awarded and, if so, the reputation of the body which awards it.

Differences also arise in organisational structures in which people are employed. Different types of line management can lead to problems when workers are trying to liaise across agencies. Social workers may have management which is very much along the lines of supporting, commenting, discussing problems, whereas health workers are more likely to have an instructive, authoritarian type of line management. Linked to this is the different hierarchical structure within each agency; education has a relatively flat structure compared to that of the health service where hierarchies within hierarchies exist (medical, nursing, auxiliary). Both these factors have implications for the extent of individuals' decision-making power and the authority they have to make decisions which will lead to changes in their own and their agency's procedures. Where some have such powers and others do not, agreements are naturally more difficult to achieve.

Each of the 'professional differences' described in the preceding sections were found to cause difficulties in a range of situations. Often they were exacerbated by personal jealousies and inter-agency competition for limited funding for client groups with special needs. The following examples are just a few of many which were encountered. They demonstrate just how intertwined the different problems posed by inter-agency working are. Thus, in the first example, professional rivalries, different expectations and failure to understand each other's terminology all arose. In the second, disagreements over language, different models of support and competition for funding made cooperation extremely difficult.

## EXAMPLE

When a local FE college became involved in the Care in the Community initiative two crucial points emerged: the participants underestimated the difficulties arising from professional differences between the agencies involved and, linked to this, they underestimated the staff training which would be needed.

Initially problems started to manifest themselves in what were described as 'personality conflicts'. The college special needs coordinator felt that the cause of the problem was a lack of understanding of each agency's role. There were many examples of this. One issue was linked to the difference in work patterns and apparently different priorities of college staff and social workers. College staff resented the fact that social workers assumed they could be released from their regular teaching commitments to attend case conferences, even at short notice. Not only could tutors not be freed easily, they also saw their primary responsibility to be that of teaching and were unhappy that case conferences were being seen as part of their departmental responsibilities and expected to take priority. Linked to this, difficulties often cropped up because of differences in status, conditions and pay.

A specific problem arose between tutors and social workers when a special needs tutor whose post had been funded by Care in the Community left the college. Social services decided not to replace him. College staff were upset by this, feeling that it demonstrated a lack of understanding of how important the post had been, and undervalued the work the tutor had been doing. The problem soured relations to such an extent that a high level joint education and social services committee was set up, chaired by the deputy director of social services and attended by social workers, education department managers and college staff.

As a result of these discussions, there was a widening of the brief of the group to look at other aspects of the college's involvement. The social services department requested a breakdown of how the college spent the money it had been allocated from Care in the Community funding for clients from long-stay hospitals. It emerged that social services were concerned that college was not giving value for money because so few Care in the Community clients were being provided for by college courses (30 of the 120 Care in the Community clients were attending college). The college did not think it was helpful to headcount in this way; it saw itself as providing a service to the whole community, of which adult special educational needs represented just one part.

Moreover, the discussions revealed that social workers and education staff had been operating under different sets of assumptions; terms such as 'rights' and 'access to education' were found to have different meanings for the different professional groups involved, indicating that they had never properly understood each other's objectives. A clear example of this emerged in the procedures for new college students arriving under the Care in the Community initiative. Each student with severe learning difficulties had been allocated a named tutor in the college whose responsibility it was to provide support and help with negotiations with other college personnel. It appeared social workers were critical of this procedure, seeing it as differentiating the student and preventing free 'access' to the whole college. The college staff, for their part, were puzzled that social workers should prefer to have students 'thrown in at the deep end', without individualised support. They believed they were facilitating 'access', not blocking it.

This led the group to set about a review of the different agencies' special needs philosophies. However, once again communication became the issue: the group became bogged down over debates such as whether 'normalisation' (social services) and 'integration' (education) meant the same thing.

## EXAMPLE

Individuals working in another area came up against the same type of problem over language. One social services manager described having prolonged clashes with the health service over the concept of 'normalisation'. He felt that the health service tended to be more protective of clients - 'a caring model' - while the social services were more inclined to take risks in order to push the client forward. A battle over funding for respite care in a local hospital became the focus of this argument. This led, eventually, to managers from health and social services participating in a three-day series of discussions to 'come to a unanimous view as to how everything should work'. This was followed up by a course organised by the British Medical Association which aimed to unite managers across the various hierarchies of different services.

## Job insecurity

Another element relating to professional differences is job insecurity. Developing inter-agency initiatives and new work patterns can seem to pose a threat to individual workers or groups of workers, particularly if in the process 'their' clients become the responsibility of other professionals. Although no criticism is usually intended, it is easy to see how feelings of resentment over loss of control or status can develop and how suspicion about future job security can hinder good working relationships being formed.

### EXAMPLE

In one area the closure of a social services SEC was at the heart of the disagreements which arose between agencies. There was a good deal of job insecurity and staff dissatisfaction among workers at the SEC over the closure. These people saw the education department's involvement as a provider of day services as little more than a 'take-over bid' which would result in the end in them losing their jobs. They were also very critical of the type of provision being made by college staff for 'their' clients, failing to see that it offered anything different to that which was offered at the SEC. Both the health service representative and the social services representative could see some basis for these concerns, and felt that the problem lay in not preparing the SEC workers sufficiently about the whole initiative. In turn this had stunted opportunities for joint working at grass roots level between FE and SEC staff; thus the opportunity to prepare for the students' transition was lost and the success of providing education and training which differed from that provided by the SEC became hit or miss.

# Exchange of information

Exchanging information about clients can be a bone of contention, even where other aspects of inter-agency working are going well. Obviously professionals have responsibility for maintaining confidentiality and clients have a right to this. Sometimes, however, workers suspect that information of a non-confidential nature is being withheld as a means of retaining a degree of control/authority. Careful negotiation over what really is and is not necessary seems to be important. Also, a system of gatekeeping whereby only key people have access to information may be worth considering.

### EXAMPLE

The problem of exchanging information arose for one college in connection with its links with the hospitals. Without regular meetings about the clients, the college was reliant on written information which, though promised, was rarely sent. The reasons for this appeared again to relate to pressure of work, but also to a certain lack of trust about how the information would be used. The problem arose, too, between the college and the SECs. The SECs seemed satisfied that what the clients passed on about themselves was the best guide; they did not think it appropriate to pass on other information. However, the college coordinator said that individual students were not always fully responsible and, in her experience, sometimes passed on incorrect information or omitted to say something vital. For example, the college did not know about a certain student's epilepsy. When this person had an epileptic fit while attending a lecture the tutor was put off having another student. The student was on a mainstream course with a tutor whom the coordinator had worked hard with to get him to accept one of her students. She felt that the tutor would not have reacted so badly had she been able to prepare him properly for such an eventuality. Thus the damage to internal college relations was an unnecessary spin-off from the SEC refusing to pass on this kind of medical information.

### EXAMPLE

A similar problem arose in another college in relation to students' case histories. The social workers were reluctant to pass any of this information on to college staff on the grounds of confidentiality. Tutors, however, felt that they needed this background knowledge, that students' behaviour would be better understood in a historical context and that problems could arise when tutors were not fully informed. An attempt was made to alleviate the problem after a great deal of negotiation, by introducing a system of 'gatekeeping'. A named senior social worker was to be contacted by the college special needs coordinator if the college team felt that information was needed about a particular student. It was then the responsibility of the nominated senior social worker to decide, having looked at the file, whether any of the information needed to be passed on to the college coordinator. If this happened, the college coordinator had in turn to decide if any tutors needed to be advised of any of the information. However, usually only health and safety aspects were communicated and college staff still felt that unfortunate incidents had arisen which might have been avoided had more been known about the student's background.

# Finding time

Finding time for inter-agency collaboration is difficult. Although in some instances lack of time can be an excuse, it is usually a very real problem for workers in already stretched services. It requires a commitment on the part of individuals, not only in terms of time but also flexibility, since different working patterns and locations make it hard to find mutually convenient times and places to meet. Moreover, when liaison starts to bear fruit and information has to be prepared and disseminated, new patterns of working introduced and new ventures undertaken, the commitment can become too burdensome, particularly if the work becomes unevenly divided between participants.

## EXAMPLE

As a result of an approach by an educational psychologist working in a local hospital, outreach classes run by an FE college special needs coordinator began. The following September a link course was arranged for selected clients to attend the college two days a week. However, a problem arose in that the hospital staff seemed relieved to have absented themselves of the responsibility for the clients attending college and liaison between the staff at the hospital and the college became minimal. Pressure of work seemed to be the main obstacle - something beyond the control of either the hospital or college staff.

## EXAMPLE

A school for pupils with severe learning difficulties was once part of the local psychiatric hospital and was based in the hospital grounds. It was decided that the school should come under the auspices of the education department and meetings between hospital and education staff were arranged to discuss the transition. However, bad feeling arose because of the different expectations of teachers and nurses in terms of making time to attend these meetings: nursing staff could not attend meetings when they were on duty, but when they were off duty they were not expected to have to work (i.e. attend meetings) whereas teachers **were** expected to give up their own time to attend the meetings after work.

# Sustaining the dialogue

Once liaison has been established, maintaining contact is a major issue. The problem associated with maintaining contact earlier in this chapter related to key people moving on, but there are other difficulties which arise. Sometimes individuals fail to recognise the importance of maintaining contact once initiatives are under way, or there is a lack of clarity about the purpose of the liaison in the first place, which can become a crucial issue when seeking to maintain dialogue. The two examples below illustrate such situations.

### EXAMPLE

In one area, the local FE college had secured Care in the Community funding to run a course for 30 people with severe learning difficulties who usually attended an SEC. At first there had been numerous meetings between the college tutors and the SEC staff to set up the course, but after a year these had ceased. The college tutors did not seem unduly worried that there was no longer any communication, even though some of their students attended both the college and the SEC on a weekly basis. However, their community services team (CST) were requested by the Care in the Community joint care planning team to conduct a review of the college provision for these students. It had this to say about liaison:

*The team feel that communication between the college and other agencies such as (the SEC), ourselves, Mencap and social workers is very important. In particular the team would like to see formal links forged between the college and (the SEC) for those part-time students who attend both establishments. Perhaps this could come to fruition via a student review system held in the college or (the SEC), or simply by nominating an instructor from (the SEC) or the college to act as a liaison officer.*

## EXAMPLE

One liaison group involved the following people:
College special needs coordinator
Two lecturers from the college's 16-19 special needs annexe
Two teachers from a linked SLD school
Speech therapist (NHS)
Community care manager (social services)
Three psychologists from the local mental hospital (NHS)
Manager of the local day centre (social services)
Senior social worker, based at the day centre
Activities organiser from a local voluntary centre which is run by an independent charity
Community placement officer (social services)
Mencap district officer
Community education officer, special measures
County special needs coordinator, post 16.

The group had been in existence for just over a year. This initial period had been used to get to know more about the job of each member of the group; a process generally felt to have been useful. However, concerns were expressed by individual members of the group about its role. Beyond the initial objective of forming a support network they had not set any specific goals. One member commented that the group was 'a toothless animal' and that part of the motivation to attend was loyalty to a concept which they knew to be right: liaison. Others felt that it was time to define a clear role before interest started to decline. Several members of the group indicated a concern that beyond information sharing, which was of some help to each other, the group had not done very much to benefit individual clients. Despite having a lot of clients in common, discussions of individuals did not seem to have been facilitated by the group's existence. The coordinator of the group felt that discussion of the progression opportunities for individuals was something which the group would achieve in time, once relationships had been consolidated. However, other members of the group did not see its purpose as becoming a forum for discussion of this type. Instead they saw its goal as one of joint planning of services for people with severe learning difficulties, even though it was recognised that the group had limited capabilities in terms of decision-making power.

However, the following example shows how dialogue can be usefully maintained, and highlights the importance of focusing attention on individual needs, particularly at transition stages. The experiences of these professionals suggest that inter-agency collaboration does not necessarily need to be a continuous process, but can be successful if the framework is in place for workers to tap into resources and opportunities at key points and in relation to individual needs.

## EXAMPLE

The first full time course for 19 year olds with learning difficulties started at the college three years earlier. The college coordinator saw multi-agency collaboration as an essential aspect of the course, involving FE staff, social services staff, special school staff, health authority staff, SEC staff, and the specialist careers adviser. Where students already had social workers, college staff liaised very closely with them. Similarly they were in touch with doctors, physiotherapists and so on. Also, the assessment procedure adopted by the college was designed to fit in with the individual programme plans (IPPs) used by social services and the health service. Towards the end of the course, the inter-agency element arose again via the social services key workers. Each of these was allocated one student for whom they had responsibility for identifying the most appropriate avenue for progression. In doing this, they were specifically required to look into four areas: education; employment; voluntary organisations; and leisure.

These, then, are some of the common, but by no means insignificant, problems which can work against successful inter-agency collaboration. We now go on to examine what steps can be taken by those attempting to resolve some of the difficulties with which they are currently faced. We suggest a number of questions that individuals, teams and whole authorities might wish to use in evaluating their practice and seeking possible ways forward.

# III MAKING PROGRESS

Coherence and continuity in provision for people with special needs requires strategic planning at regional and local level. Since the Education Reform Act of 1988, LEAs have been required to incorporate within their strategic plans the requirements of post-sixteen year olds with special needs. By 1993, if the FE sector is no longer under the control of the LEAs, this coordinating role will have disappeared. It will, however, need to be replaced by some form of regional or local initiative. The ad hoc links with health and social services developed by individual practitioners will doubtless continue to meet immediate needs. They do not, however, provide an adequate basis for longer-term funding arrangements and programme planning. It must be recognised that multi-agency collaboration is in its infancy. It has reached a stage in its development when the main task is to take stock and plan for the next step.

The fact that multi-agency working has to date proved so difficult to achieve has led a number of commentators to express the view that efforts so far expended in this area may in fact have been a waste of time, that they have been more for the benefit of the professionals than the clients and that other models should now be being sought. One such model which has been gaining ground as a potential way forward is the *Danish Kurator* system whereby a young person is attached to an individual professional who acts as a continuous point of reference throughout the years of transition. The *Kurator* is required to ensure that interventions from all the relevant agencies involved at various points in a young person's life are coordinated in such a way as to implement individual action plans to best effect. Another useful model focuses squarely on the collaborative work of a small team whose role it is to ensure that individual needs are carefully identified and that individualised plans (IPP) are put into effect. The essential element of this model is the fact that planning is carried out in considerable detail so that each member of the professional team knows precisely who is doing what and when. Further information can be found in Wehman (1989).

The questions offered below are intended to focus attention on a number of considerations which have implications for successful inter-agency working. The questions are aimed either at senior management or practitioners, but inevitably there will be some overlap and each group will find it useful to consider both sections. The guidelines the questions offer are not intended to be prescriptive. This would underestimate the complexity of inter-agency working which requires a great deal of individual negotiation and consultation, taking on board local situations and historical arrangements. The purpose of phrasing the section as a series of questions is to encourage individuals or groups within services to ask themselves how well their existing collaborative arrangements are working in terms of supporting people with special needs. The questions are inevitably general, and it is for individuals to develop their implications as they relate to their particular situation.

Before embarking on these checklists it is worth giving some time to thinking why collaborative working is necessary, why you wish to become involved in it and who will benefit from your efforts. The answer to all these questions should be the individual who needs your support. While multi-agency collaboration may be a part of your job, an intellectual and practical challenge to your professionalism, for the person who has special needs it can open the door to life chances which otherwise would remain closed.

## SELF EVALUATION CHECKLIST FOR SENIOR MANAGERS

### Inter-agency policy development

- Does your service have a special needs policy?
- Is the policy written down?
- When was policy last reviewed?
- When do you plan to review it again?
- How do you monitor the implementation of the policy?
- Do you consider the policy to be adequately resourced?
- If you do not have a policy, how are decisions about special needs provision made?
- Do you have a copy of other services' policy documents on special needs?
- How do you coordinate your work with that of other services, avoiding both duplication and gaps in provision for people with special needs?
- Have there been any attempts to negotiate agreement with other service providers about special needs policy?

- When did your service last review its provision for people with special needs?

- How do you liaise with peers in other services?

- How are issues of common concern to the various services brought to senior management attention?

- How effective are these current procedures in terms of coordinating service provision?

- Are you satisfied that workers in your service are working well with those in other services?

- Do you know of any support networks or working parties with multi-professional representation?

- Have attempts been made to rationalise these in order to avoid duplication of effort?

- Are networks involving different professionals actively encouraged/supported through

  - joint policy agreement?

  - established procedures for maintaining an updated record of who is involved, their role and responsibilities?

  - structures for networks to feed back information to their own service hierarchy?

  - structures to facilitate joint working?

  - provision of resources?

- Concerning such groups, how much do you know about objectives, issues under discussion, problems encountered and documentation produced?

- How do you ensure that the work of such groups is not being reproduced elsewhere?

- How is information on the existence and work of such groups disseminated within your service, beyond service boundaries and to clients?

## Keeping links going

- Is it possible to make any changes in terms of local authority structures, funding arrangements and strategic planning to facilitate and encourage joint working initiatives at every level?

- Have issues concerning areas of responsibility been addressed and steps taken to rationalise these?

- Have workers in the different services been fully consulted about proposed changes in areas of responsibility and their views taken into account?

- Can anything be done about potential difficulties arising from differences in conditions of service between different professional groups (e.g. reviewing job descriptions, ensuring that time is allocated for liaison, consultation before introducing new initiatives)?

- Are lines of communication adequate to cope with cross service needs as well as within service needs, thus avoiding the negative impact of rumour and uncertainty where adequate communication is lacking?

- Have ways of securing joint rather than separate funding been explored fully?

- Have the cost implications of implementing joint working policies been addressed?

- Has the issue of joint training been tackled
  - in terms of circulation of information concerning training?
  - in terms of funding arrangements?
  - in terms of course content/language/location?

- Are recommendations arising from network groups lower down the hierarchy discussed by inter-agency representatives at senior management level?

## SELF EVALUATION CHECKLIST FOR PRACTITIONERS

### Inter-agency policy development

- In the absence of senior level policy development, have you drawn up your own policy statement on aims and objectives for clients with special needs?

- Have you included, as far as possible, agreement over any practical aspects which have presented problems in the past? (The elements which you may need to consider are confidentiality, who attends student reviews, when these take place, exchange of client information, communication with parents, curriculum content and so on.)

- Is the size and composition of the policy-making group appropriate? (Holding large meetings to draw up guidelines is likely to result in wide-ranging and possibly fragmented discussions which achieve little.)

- Have all interested parties had a say in any new policies or procedures being proposed? (A useful strategy seems to be the creation of a core group to draw up DRAFT recommendations which can then be circulated for comment to as many people as necessary, including clients and parents.)

- Are agreements which have been made written down?

- Where are they kept? Who has access to them? Does the authority 'own' them?

- Does EVERYONE who is likely to be influenced either in their work or life by the agreements know about the policy you have drawn up? Better still, do they have a written copy?

---

## Starting up links

*Identifying aims and objectives*

- Have aims and objectives for the group been discussed fully?

- Do you share common goals for the meetings/liaison itself?

- What are you doing about people who don't agree?

- Have agreed aims and objectives been written down coherently?

- Do colleagues in your own sector know about the group and its goals?

- Do they agree with these goals?

## Identifying the right people

- Can you think of other people who ought to be invited to join the group?

- Does your job remit in terms of clients span the same area as others in the group?

- Do members of the group encompass the range of services and/or knowledge of provision needed?

- Is the group becoming too large - will its size encourage or discourage discussion?

## Starting point for discussion

- At the early meetings, are you prepared to
  - identify target clients?
  - discuss your job and role within your service?
  - exchange copies of job descriptions?
  - exchange information on agency procedures and limits of individuals' power to act?
  - reach agreements over confidentiality?

- Have your colleagues been consulted about your involvement in the group?

- Do they support this?

- What happens to decisions reached within the network which have wider implications than the day-to-day work of individual practitioners within the group?

- Is the structure in place to enable you to feed back your conclusions into the authority hierarchy of decision-making?

## Organisation

- Is there an adequate system of maintaining up-to-date information on roles and responsibilities of individuals within the network?

- Is the organisation of the meetings satisfactory for everyone concerned?
  - timing of meetings
  - location of meetings
  - not enough structure/too much structure to meetings
  - agenda
  - minutes (are they needed, who does them, are they circulated?)

- Is attendance at the meetings stable/improving/declining?

- Is liaison with the other members of the group recognised as part of the individual's responsibility and is this written into the job description together with appropriate time allocation?

- Would it be appropriate for other members of the same team to share attendance at the meetings to avoid one person feeling overburdened?

- Would shared attendance prove too fragmented, indicating a need for a rotating responsibility or for official time to be given to the person whose job it is to liaise?

- How could new people taking up post tap into the network?

### Working relationships

- Do you feel your group is working well together?

- Is there anything you feel unhappy about in connection with the initial period of information exchange (i.e. still unsure about/do not think it appropriate in terms of an individual's job)?

- Do group members share common goals for the same client groups?

- Are there professional differences which need resolving between individuals or groups of individuals?

- If yes, would any of the following help with this problem?
    - raising the matter for discussion within the group
    - broadening out the discussion to involve other people
    - senior management input/support/decision-making
    - joint in-service training

## *Function of the group*

- How do individual group members communicate information or decisions arising from the meetings to colleagues in their own service?

- How is the information received by these people?

- Do you have the support of your colleagues in attending these meetings?

- Have colleagues who are not involved in liaison meetings been fully consulted about any agreements made?

- Have you circulated any information arising from the group to them?

- Have the original objectives of the group been met/ partially met?

- Are objectives now perceived to be realistic or do steps need to be taken to make them more so, such as
  - inviting other people, possibly more senior people to attend?
  - gaining official recognition for the group and hence the right to feed into the system conclusions reached or issues requiring a wider audience?
  - securing management support/authority for decisions?
  - securing access to resources?

- Is there a need to formulate a new role for the group in view of any local developments?

- Has the time come to set a wider agenda, such as development of joint initiatives to support people with special needs?

### Curriculum issues

- Has curriculum documentation been exchanged with other members of the network?

- Has the group been involved in talking about the curriculum?

- What are the difficulties in trying to talk about the curriculum?

- What benefits have arisen from curriculum discussions with workers in other locations/services?

- Have any agreements been made to ensure curriculum continuity either side of transfer?

- Have any such agreements been written down?

- Has there been full consultation within institutions before changes were agreed?

- Is there a need for in-service training in relation to curriculum issues e.g. for non-education service workers?

### Evaluation

- What strategies have you employed so far to evaluate the liaison/work of the network?

- What have been the positive outcomes so far?

- What aspects have proved negative?

- Have most of the original aims been achieved?

- Are there new aims which need to be set?

- Has the position, nationally or locally affected what you have been doing in any way?

- How have you tackled this?

- Has a need for joint training been identified?


## SOME FURTHER SUGGESTIONS FOR ESTABLISHED GROUPS

If your group is working well together but problems still exist which are linked to lack of senior management support/policy development, it is probably the right time to attempt to tackle this. The best you can hope to achieve, realistically, is awareness-raising. Draw attention to the fact that there is no inter-agency policy at local authority level. Provide concrete examples of problems which commonly occur through not having joint policy agreements at senior level, such as difficulties with transport arrangements, curriculum discontinuity, who attends student reviews, missed opportunities for those with special needs, duplication of effort, gaps in service provision, confusion for clients and parents/carers. How do you communicate these points? The best approach seems likely to be a several-pronged attack, but it will obviously depend very much on local circumstances and the resources of the group as to how any of the following suggestions are taken up or adapted:

- Write to senior local authority officers.

- Seek a meeting with senior officers to discuss some of the problems arising from a lack of joint policy development.

- Try to gain access to senior managers' ears through existing channels of communication, e.g. departmental planning meetings, council meetings, Care in the Community meetings. Depending on protocol, the liaison group could ask for an item to be added to the agenda and send a paper or, perhaps, representatives.

- Use existing contacts/lines of communication, e.g. line managers, to put forward some of the issues. Winning over 'converts' at the next level up from you is a step in the right direction.

- Organise a local conference or training day, focusing on issues to do with policy development and cooperative working and invite senior people to attend.

These suggestions for self evaluation are intended to offer food for thought to those who have no experience of liaison across agency boundaries and to serve as a springboard for review for those who have. They are based on the experiences and problems encountered by others working in the minefield of inter-agency collaboration but are, of course, by no means a definitive list. Reading through the checklists may well give you many other ideas which will translate better to your own context and situation.

# REFERENCES

BRADLEY, J. and POCKLINGTON, K. (1990). *Perceptions of Special Needs in FE*. London: FEU.

CASTREE, B.J. and WALKER, J.H. (1981). 'The young adult with spina bifida', *British Medical Journal*, 283, 1040-1042.

DEPARTMENT OF EDUCATION AND SCIENCE (1991). *Transition from School to Further Education for Students with Learning Difficulties*. A Report by HMI. London: DES.

DEPARTMENT OF HEALTH (1990). *Developing Services for Young People with Disabilities: Towards Implementing Sections 5 and 6 of the Disabled Persons Act 1986*. A Report by SSI. London: Department of Health.

HIRST, M. (1983). 'Young people with disabilities: What happens after 16?' *Child: Care, Health and Development*, 9, 273-284.

HUTCHINSON, D. (1985). 'Cooperation and coordination', In: Bradley, J.,Dee, L. and Hegarty, S. *From Coping to Confidence*. Slough: NFER.

SILLS, P. (1987). 'Cooperation in staff training', paper presented to the Royal Society of Medicine Forum on Mental Rehabilitation. November, 1986.

THOMAS, A.P. *et al.* (1985). 'The health and social needs of physically handicapped young adults', *Developmental Medicine and Child Neurology*, 27,4, Supplement No. 50.

WARBURTON, R.W. (1990). *Developing Services for Disabled People: Results of an Inspection to Monitor the Operation of the Disabled Persons (Services, Consultation and Representation) Act 1986*. A report by SSI. London: Department of Health.

WEHMAN, P. *et al.* (1987). *Transition from School to Work: New Challenges for Youth with Severe Handicaps*. Baltimore: P. H. Brookes.

# OTHER PUBLICATIONS

**Other in-house publications available from the NFER include:**

The Work and Impact of Advisory Teachers

Developing the Arts in Primary Schools

The Changing Role, Structure and Style of LEAs

About Change: Schools' and LEAs' Perspectives on LEA Reorganization

Enabling Teachers to Undertake INSET

A Survey of School Governing Bodies

Towards Effective Partnerships in School Governance

Foreign Languages for Lower Attaining Pupils

Staff Appraisal: The FE Pilot Schemes

Charging for School Activities

Education: Guide to European Organizations and Programmes

Four Year Olds in School: Quality Matters

Vocational Education Opportunities for Students with Speech and Language Impairments

SACREs: Their Formation, Composition, Operation and Role on RE and Worship

Copies of these publications are obtainable from:

Editorial Services, NFER, The Mere, Upton Park, SLOUGH, SL1 2DQ